The Courage to Pray

THE COURAGE TO PRAY

Karl Rahner &
Johann Baptist Metz

Crossroad · New York

1981
The Crossroad Publishing Company
18 East 41st Street, New York, N.Y. 10017

Published originally as *Ermutigung zum Gebet* by Verlag
Herder, Freiburg im Breisgau, Federal Republic of Germany
Copyright © 1977 Verlag Herder.

Translated from the German by Sarah O'Brien Twohig. English
translation copyright © 1980 by Search Press Ltd.

Printed in the United States of America

Library of Congress Cataloging in Publication Data
Main entry under title:
The courage to pray.
    Translation of Ermutigung zum Gebet.
    "A Crossroad book."
    CONTENTS: Metz, J. B. The courage to pray.—
Rahner, K. Prayer to the saints.
    1. Prayer—Addresses, essays, lectures.
    2. Christian saints—Cult—Addresses, essays,
lectures. I. Metz, Johannes Baptist, 1928–
Ermutigung zum Gebet. English. 1980. II. Rahner,
Karl, 1904–   Gebet zu den Heiligen. English.
1980.
BV213.E7513   248.3'2   80-18594
ISBN 0-8245-0002-4   Previously ISBN 0-8164-2024-6

Contents

The Courage to Pray

One

THE COURAGE
TO PRAY

Johann Baptist Metz

Many people today no longer pray even in private. Prayer seems strange, alienating and inaccessible. We feel no inclination for it even when prayer is the only form of language that can express our lives and feelings adequately. Surely no Christian nowadays would dispute that we need the courage to pray, especially for ourselves.

1 · The Historical Solidarity of Prayer

To begin with I should like to discuss the historical solidarity of those who pray. We are not alone when we pray; we have more support than most of us realize. We are part of a great tradition which has formed our identity as human beings. This tradition stretches right back to the unknown beginnings of the history of mankind. As the German Synod text *Our Hope* says, 'The name of God is graven deeply in the history of mankind's hopes and sufferings. It brings enlightenment and is obscured, is revered and denied, misused and disgraced, yet never forgotten.'

What do we know about the history of mankind?

First and foremost we know something about the great and the mighty, about the rulers and their victories, and sometimes about their tragedies. In the past those were the facts that shaped our knowledge of history. But what about the others, the countless masses who actually won the victories for their rulers, who built the monuments and who mourned their numerous dead? What do we know about them? One thing we can say with certainty is that in their suffering and their grief, in their joy and their fear, they called to God, imploring him and admonishing him, praising him and thanking him. They prayed. Their history is the history of prayer.

The history of mankind seen as popular history is basically the history of religion, and religious history in the final analysis is the history of prayer. And this is not limited to the history of Christian Europe. It applies especially to Judaeo-Hebraic history which in turn became the foundation of history for both Christianity and Islam. It applies equally to many remote, impenetrable cultures in Asia and Africa. We Christians should have every respect for this unfamiliar history and for the validity of the hopes and sufferings it contains.

Through prayer we become part of a great historical solidarity. Prayer introduces into the history of mankind a voice that gives expression to our hope and trust. Yet the significance of this religious voice throughout the history of mankind, this silent plea for prayer from the anonymous mass of the dead, is frequently disputed. The concept of the history of mankind as the history of mankind at prayer has often been disregarded or dismissed. The dead are easily overlooked. Perhaps our attitude to the history of prayer is determined by sympathy rather than respect. We make excuses for it instead of taking it seriously: 'They didn't know any better; they had a false consciousness; they still lived in a collective darkness conditioned by archaic fears . . . Most of them were frankly credulous. But their voices cannot be included in the present dispute about humanity and its hopes. The ignorant have no competence to speak . . .' To decide who is knowledgeable and who is ignorant with respect to hope, religion and prayer is not a matter for those who have themselves lived and suffered in the light of religious experience; nor can it be decided by those who pray, the subjects of this language of prayer. Instead, the decision lies with those of us who adhere to the idea of a logical evaluation of mankind, invariably equating knowledge with more recent stages of development, and thus reducing earlier ages to the level of mass ignorance. This attitude accounts for the long-established practice of harshly and mindlessly criticizing and destroying the memories and symbols of this history of prayer. This can take many forms: through writing (a focus of apathy); in the easy comfort of lengthy reflection, protected from the irritating limitations of practical application; in the 'safe' realm of pure theory, well insulated against any apocalyptical storm, yet aware of everything, with nothing strange or unexplained, where all languages are known and spoken, with the exception of the language of suffering and hope, which is prayer.

If we are to avoid succumbing to the current illusion which equates the present with the most advanced state of human awareness, we must remind ourselves that the sum total of the living is far too small, too arbitrary, and probably also too lacking in imagination, and hence is not competent to make any final judgment about the fate of religion and prayer. Should we not therefore be more willing to extend the right to a say in matters of religion and prayer to include the dead also? Surely we must discard any superficial impression that prayer is too weak or insipid if it requires the support of the dead and the voice of tradition in order to survive.

Those who pray are part of a great historical company. The chief mainstay of this solidarity is above all the history of prayer contained in the Old Testament, and indeed that of the Jewish people. This is not without contemporary relevance, for example, in the case of Germany. Referring to the Nazi concentration camps a Jewish philosopher coined the well-known saying that after Auschwitz poetry was dead. And what about prayer? Can we take it for granted that after Auschwitz it is still possible to pray? A Marxist philosopher of religion, Milan Machoveć, felt strongly that it was not. During a debate in 1966 he asked me how, after Auschwitz, Christians still found the courage to pray. The answer I tried to give him still strikes me as the only convincing one: 'We can and should pray after Auschwitz because even in Auschwitz, in the hell of Auschwitz, they prayed'. This context links prayer in Germany, for instance, in a very special way with the history of prayer of the Jewish people. And it is an indication of the promise *and* the obligation implied in the opening words of this chapter: Those who pray are not alone; they form part of a great historical company; prayer is a matter of historical solidarity.

2 · What Is Prayer?

But what is prayer? I should like to comment on the *characteristics of prayer and the language of prayer.* Again, it is not my intention to say much 'about' prayer as such—how could one say everything that would need to be said? Rather, I wish to give people encouragement to pray.

To pray is to say Yes to God, to affirm the sense of contradiction we experience, the pain of mortality and death, the suffering caused by violence and oppression. 'I am overcome by my trouble. I am distraught by the noise of the enemy, because of the oppression of the wicked. . . . My heart is in anguish within me, the terrors of death have fallen upon me. Fear and trembling come upon me, and horror overwhelms me. And I say, "O that I had wings like a dove!" . . . But I call upon

God; and the Lord will save me' (Psalm 55).

This psalm shows that our simple definition of prayer is full of tension and drama. In no way is the difficulty of saying Yes concealed or glossed over with false confidence. The great tradition of prayer in the Old Testament—in the psalms, in Job, in the lamentations of the prophets—makes it clear that the language of prayer does not exclude or shut itself off from the experience of suffering and desolation. On the contrary, it is the language of pain and crisis, of lament and accusation; it is the grumbling and outcry of the children of Israel. 'Therefore I will not restrain my mouth; I will speak in the anguish of my spirit; I will complain in the bitterness of my soul' (Job 7). The language of prayer is that of our impassioned questioning of God and hence also expresses our tensely anxious expectation that God will one day vindicate the terrible suffering of the world. Protest is fused with unreserved lament, and the tenderness of the language in no way denies its sadness.

The language of prayer does not express joy either patronizingly or peremptorily. Nor is it submissive like the language of a servant to his master. Those who pray are certainly neither weak yes-men nor bound by compulsive obedience; they are neither cowards nor piously subservient. The very nature of the language of prayer throughout ʳhe Old Testament contradicts that attitude.

Again and again prayer is a cry of lament from the depths of the spirit. But this cry is in no sense a vague, rambling moan. It calls out loudly, insistently. Nor is it merely a wish or a desire, no matter how fervent. It is a supplication. The language of prayer finds its purpose and justification in the silently concealed face of God. Hence the lament, supplication, crying and protest contained in prayer, as also the silent accusation of the wordless cry, can never simply be translated and dissolved into a discourse.

Precisely because it cannot be translated, the language of prayer is so comprehensive and liberating. No other form of language is so free from linguistic constraints. Nothing is excluded, be it doubt, resignation, protest or rejection, provided that the individual wishes to turn to God and to seek his confidence. We can tell God everything: all our suffering, our doubt, even our doubt about our faith in him and about his hearing us when we turn to him. In this sense the Old Testament language of prayer is full of formulations somewhat daunting to the ordinary Christian. In fact they demonstrate that these prayers are alive. Prayer does not restrain or constrain the language of suffering; rather it extends it immeasurably, ineffably.

Christian prayer should always retain this quality. Christians have all too frequently given the impression that their religion is based on a plethora of answers and too few impassioned questions. But Christianity is much more than a religion of dogmas. And Christian prayer is certainly not a game of questions and answers. We need only to look at Jesus and his prayer to see this. Jesus' prayer, very briefly, culminates in his cry to the Father for having forsaken him. The degree of acquiescence and obedience contained in this cry reflects the measure of his suffering. His suffering came from God. His prayer from the cross is the cry of one forsaken by God, yet of one who has never deserted God. This suffering is different again from the expression of solidarity with the misery of the world. There is nothing noble about this suffering, nothing of the sublimity of love that must suffer impotently. In the words of the Bible, it is the suffering of the desolate. This is the spirit in which Jesus says yes and dies in affirmation. The mysticism of suffering embodied in the prayers of the Old Testament is not suppressed or diminished. On the contrary it is grasped at its very roots.

3 · Approaches to Prayer

Prayer is not a desperate attempt to pull ourselves out of the abyss. We gain the strength to pray from Christ's prayer. 'Following in the steps of Jesus we must live according to the poverty of his obedience. Through prayer we dare to offer our lives unconditionally to the Father'. At this point I should like to comment on the different approaches to this kind of prayer.

There is for example the *prayer of fear*. Praying is not an imaginary ladder enabling us to escape from our fears. Nor does it suppress or overcome our fears. First and foremost it permits fear. 'My soul is very sorrowful, even to death', Christ prayed in the Garden of Gethsemane (cf. Matt. 26:38). Fear is allowed in, not banished. Fear, sorrow and distress can easily provide the impetus to pray. Apathy has

no part to play in prayer. The aim of prayer is not to
protect us from pain or suffering. Nothing alarms
us more than a person ostensibly devoid of fear.
But is it not true that fear makes people malleable
and unfree; that frightened people are precisely
those most liable to be exploited by outside forces?
We must be more specific. Only when fear is suppressed do we become unfree and manipulated;
only then can fear constrict our hearts and render
us incapable of conceiving our own anguish or that
of those around us. By means of prayer, however,
this fear can even make us free, just as Christ was
freed by his fearful prayer of distress in the Garden
of Olives.

Then there is *prayer induced by guilt.* Again
prayer can prevent us from giving in to the web of
excuses we weave around ourselves; it can help us
cope with the misery of our guilty consciences.
What can we feel if, reflecting on the past, we have
to admit to ourselves that our lives are scattered
with the ruins of people destroyed by our egoism?
Faced with such a realization, what reaction could
we have but an overwhelming desire to make
amends? What alternative is there to despair but
the plea for forgiveness and, according to the mes-
sianic light of hope, additional pleas precisely for
those destroyed? This argument is of course open
to the suspicion that our religious outcry in reaction
to our own guilt amounts to a very subtle form of

escapism, both from ourselves and from responsibility. I shall return later to the idea that prayer incorporates the readiness to accept responsibility. At this point I should like to draw attention to a number of ways of approaching the mystical aspect of prayer.

The examples given above might possibly suggest that the way to prayer is through negative experiences, through pain, sorrow and distress, rather than through the positive influence of joy and gratitude. In reality, however, the active fight against overwhelming hopelessness, affirmation in the negative face of pain, is the outcome of a tremendously positive attitude. The experience of prayer I wish to underline here has a long tradition in the history of religion and especially in the history of our own faith. In history prayer is not limited to the expression of joy and exaltation; on the contrary, it also embraces the expression of fear and despair, a cry from the depths of the soul.

For this reason I should like to mention a danger which I feel is implicit in the customary language of prayer currently used by the Church. Perhaps not enough emphasis is laid on the pain of negativity? Perhaps our prayers are often much too positive and over-affirmative, resorting to clichés when referring to suffering and conflict and thus incapable of giving adequate expression to our acceptance of difficulties and crises? In my view this kind of prayer is symptomatic of weakness and despondency, and no longer entrusts our pain and the despair of our lives to God in prayer.

This tendency to be overly affirmative in our daily prayers is full of serious implications. It surely exacerbates our inarticulateness in pain and crises, depressing us further instead of giving us courage. How can people in dangerous situations, in pain or oppression, identify with prayers which use this kind of language? And how can this language be combined with those 'traces of prayer' which can still be found even in our so-called 'post-religious age'? I mean here the powerless rebellion against overwhelming meaninglessness, the lament and elegy which manage to survive in spite of the suppression of sadness and melancholy in contemporary society, and the cry for justice for unexpiated suffering.

It is precisely because of this absence of suffering in the official Christian language of prayer that we generally fail to notice what 'modern humanity' loses with the gradual impoverishment of the language of prayer. The disappearance of this language of prayer means, in the most literal sense, that we have lost the only language capable of expressing many situations and experiences in our lives.

4 · Prayer and Politics

At this point I must turn to the *purpose and function
of prayer* 'in the spirit of Christ'. The underlying
mysticism of this kind of prayer is evident. It entails
a shift in responsibility, both social and political.
'Christ's obedience is also the source of his particular love for mankind, his closeness to the humble,
the rejected, the sinners and the desolate' (from the
German Synod text *Our Hope*).

If we are to pray 'in the spirit of Christ" we cannot turn our backs on the sufferings of others.
Prayer demands that we love our fellow humans;
we have no choice. It can make prayer extremely
dangerous, for example, in situations where humanity is systematically suppressed and people are
forced to live as though no bonds of allegiance
existed between them. This need for humanity

urges Christians today to adopt a positive attitude towards prayer. We must pray not just *for* the poor and unfortunate but *with* them. This contradicts our instinctive tendency to avoid the company of those who are unhappy or suffering. If we pray 'in his spirit' we can afford to be despised by those who consider themselves to be intelligent and enlightened; but not by those who are disconsolate, suffering or oppressed. And this means that prayer is of necessity political and influential.

Hence we must take care not to let our prayers turn into a eulogistic evasion of what really matters, serving merely to lift the apathy from our souls and our indifference and lack of sympathy towards other people's suffering. Let us consider the language of our 'modern' prayers of petition which often purport to be 'explicit' and 'social' in intent. Are they really prayers or merely excuses by which we take the easy option, with little risk of responsibility? 'Lord help drug addicts back to a "normal" life' or 'Lord help prevent racial discrimination, and give food to the poor countries of the third world . . .' Surely the only practical effect of such prayers can be to appease our consciences. A mature attitude towards prayer presupposes the readiness to assume responsibility. And it feeds on the contradictory, painful feelings which necessarily accompany the acceptance and fulfilment of this responsibility.

This practical and political aspect of prayer is also highly relevant in a religious sense. We should face up to our fears and doubts and consider in all seriousness the nature of the God to whom we direct our prayers. Is this silent, faceless God not an indifferent idol, a Baal, a Moloch? Is he not an unbearable tyrant enthroned in an elevated realm to which our longings and sufferings have no entry? Is he not the reflection and sealing of a feudalistic master-slave relationship, the last remnant of an obsolete, archaic system of sovereignty? Perhaps the mysticism of prayer leads to misanthropic masochism? Surely prayer poisons our hard-won freedom of consciousness with further archaic fears and constraints? With such questions in mind it is important to study the prayers of Christ himself. The God of his prayers is 'our Father' too; his prayers, his whole demeanour, his entire destiny make this evident. From this we can see clearly that the God of his prayers is neither a humiliating tyrant nor the projection of worldly power and authority. Rather, he is the God of insuperable love, the God of a dwelling almost beyond our imagining, the God who wipes away our tears and gathers lost souls into the radiant clasp of his mercy. Hence as followers of Christ we must continually make it clear, both to ourselves and to others, to whom we are praying and whom we mean when we say 'God'. The qualities of this liberating, edifying God to whom we pray must be visible in our conduct and attitudes.

There can be no universally effective theoretical contradiction of the suspicion that prayer is the opium of the people, or indeed that it is intended specifically for the people and is the classical expression of a false consciousness. Nor can we successfully use 'pure theory' to counter attempts to deprive prayer of its authenticity by adapting it to the functional systems of a liberal society, treating it as a welcome means of absorbing socially generated disappointments and frustrations: in short, regarding prayer as a useful social tool to ensure the smooth running of society. The only effective stand we can take against such attacks is to be active followers of Christ, who in his prayers called God his 'Father' and ours.

5 · Prayer as Meditation

What does prayer remind us of? The answer, perhaps surprisingly, is that prayer reminds us of *ourselves*. This is all the odder, given that we spend more and more time trying to forget ourselves. Because of the highly complex, largely anonymous social systems in which we live there is a real danger of our identity being lost, of our dreams and fantasies being reduced to nothing, of our being reduced to the level of expedient animals and machines functioning smoothly in the name of evolution and technology. This so-called progress surely has a very damaging effect on what we call our self-awareness. We feel powerless in the face of a grimly sinister universe, and drawn into an anonymous evolution which engulfs each of us mercilessly. 'As for man, his days are like grass; he flourishes like a flower of the field; for the wind passes over it, and it is gone, and its place knows it no more' (Psalm 103). What we are undergoing today is surely an extension on a universal scale of this experience from the nomadic world of the Old Testament. At the same time our primitive fear of losing our name is also increasing. Thus we can see the contemporary relevance of the Old Testament prayer: 'The Lord called me from the womb, from the body of my mother he named my name' (Isaiah 49:1). In saying Yes to God we are reminded of ourselves. Prayer is the oldest form of the human battle for subjectivity and identity against all odds.

Prayer reminds us in particular of *childhood*. It is like returning to our own childhood, to its feeling of confidence but also to its unanswered questions and longings. Somehow prayer always retains the difficulties of childhood. Yet this childlike quality reveals that the spontaneity of prayer has as little to do with artificial or dubious naïveté as it has with spontaneous existential optimism. In this context I should like to risk adapting a famous phrase of Ernst Bloch's (stemming originally, he has stated, from an ancient Indian tradition) to prayer: Prayer is at times like the daydream of that home whose light shines in our childhood, yet a home where none of us has ever been.

6 · Prayer as Resistance

Finally, I wish to consider what prayer is *reacting against,* to see prayer as an alternative attitude in our personal and daily lives. Prayer is really an act of opposition.

Prayer opposes the threatening banality of our lives. It resists the debasement of human life to a society focussed on needs and consumerism, in which the ability to mourn and to celebrate declines because needs can only be fulfilled, not celebrated, and because mourning is quite literally valueless. Prayer, as stressed previously, is not a question-and-answer game; nor is it to be seen as barter. God does speak, but he does not give answers and almost never repeats himself. Prayer makes our questions seem questionable; it alienates our wishes; it reassesses our interests. It removes us from the vicious circle of question and answer, of means and end.

Prayer is an assault on the prevailing apathy with which we consistently and increasingly protect ourselves against hurt and disappointment until we finally reach the stage where nothing can touch us any more. In the face of these widespread identity fears I see a new stoicism emerging which, in order to avoid having to experience pain, refuses to acknowledge life as a struggle. Insensibility will be the rubric of this new cult. Apathy far more than hatred has a destructive effect than even hate on religion and prayer. It is also worse for oneself and for one's future in a human society based on freedom and solidarity. The moderate feelings of our day-to-day existence can scarcely be of any help here. We need to be stirred up by more extreme emotions: we need a prayer that embodies these feelings, that does not suppress them in any way but activates them against the gradual dominance of apathy. (It is bad enough that our traditional form of prayer has not really evolved a language suitable to express this. For example, where would we find a language of mourning in which the mourner does not deny his grief, but rather expresses it himself?)

In the final analysis prayer is a resistance to that particular kind of hopelessness and resignation which takes root in our highly developed consciousness no matter how often we dismiss it rationally or pragmatically. This hopelessness is exactly the right prerequisite for our kind of technically and pragmatically orientated rationality. Its calculating logic presupposes a concept of time as an endless, constant continuum. Perhaps the feeling of being locked into an infinite, empty, anonymous time—called 'evolution'—has long since extinguished any substantial sense of hope or expectation. Do we still know what it means to wait in anticipation for something? Not for the individual at a given time in the world, but for this time itself, for the world as a whole. All of us must surely have experienced this feeling. The radio announcer gives a brief, matter-of-fact report about some shattering catastrophe, and the music begins again. It is as though the music were an acoustic metaphor for the course of time, halted by nothing, submerging everything mercilessly and endlessly. Or can we see it differently?

Prayer is a source of opposition, an 'intermission', a means of resistance to that inexorable continuity which reduces us to apathy and makes us so apolitical (as will be borne out by the technocratic future of our societies), and so makes us incapable of expecting anything. Samuel Beckett's *Waiting for Godot* is not a play which would easily lend itself to a theological adaptation as an eschatological drama about the anticipation of God. It does not say anything about God, but in my view it does deal with 'waiting' or rather with this epoch's 'inability to anticipate or expect anything'. Perhaps Christians have also drifted into this unfortunate state? 'Again and again we continue to claim that we are waiting and watching for the Lord. But if we were honest with ourselves, we should have to admit that we no longer expect anything' (Teilhard de Chardin).

Prayer can and must be the source which renews this expectation. It must stir us up against that annihilating hopelessness which undermines any commitment based on an ulterior motive. Hence Christianity's oldest prayer is simultaneously the most up-to-date: 'Come, Lord Jesus!' (Rev. 22:20).

Two

PRAYER TO
THE SAINTS

Karl Rahner

The following reflections on prayer to the saints are based on the official liturgical veneration of saints in the Catholic Church and on the Church's teaching and practice. Hence I shall refer primarily to those who, according to official church procedures, are publicly venerated as 'saints' by the Church. But I should also include all the dead who have gone to rest in God, the blissful consummation of their earthly existence. And since we cannot, indeed should not, exclude anyone definitively from the hope of eternal happiness, I really must extend the discussion to include prayer to all the deceased. This is in no way to deny the legitimate distinction between the Church's official veneration of the saints and the individual's private prayer that can be addressed to all the deceased.

Extending the theme in this way raises certain issues which ought to be discussed about the invocation of the saints and the assumptions on which it is based. On the other hand, this approach is hardly surprising in the context of Catholic practice and teaching, given that the faithful have always prayed to the souls of the departed, without the express approval of the magisterium of the Church and against the opinions of Thomas Aquinas.

1 · It Is 'Good and Beneficial' to Pray to the Saints

The Church's teaching on this issue is summed up in Ludwig Ott's words: 'It is permissible and beneficial to venerate the saints in heaven and to ask them for their intercession'. That is the doctrine of the Council of Trent. The Second Vatican Council (e.g., *Lumen Gentium,* 50f.) admits unequivocally and as self-evident the invocation and veneration of saints which began with the veneration of the early Christian martyrs, though it does warn against the misuse or exaggeration of the practice. The dictum of the Council of Trent that it is 'good and beneficial' to invoke the help of the saints does not however impose on Christians any duty to do so. Rather, it is intended (not unlike indulgences) to give them a measure of freedom in their spiritual lives; they are free to pray to the saints—or not—if they wish.

How is this prayer to the saints actually practised today? The Church is an immensely complex structure, owing to the many different cultures it embraces throughout the world, through the greatly diverging levels of general and religious education it contains, and because of the inconsistency of consciousness and the variance in culturally and socially conditioned attitudes it contains. It is thus not possible to find one answer to this question that will be applicable to the whole Church. This is not even feasible with reference to those members of the Church who are committed Christians dedicated to a life of intense Christian piety. There are certainly a great many people (though this will differ from one country to the next) who regard praying to the saints as a matter of course, convinced of its validity as a religious experience even without further official proof or justification.

But does this apply everywhere and to all Catholic Christians who seriously wish to practise their faith? Or can those quite committed Christians who do not pray to the saints be reassured that to be good Christians they do not have to do so and are in no way bound to maintain any such relationship with the dead? Christianity today is going through a very difficult phase in which it is necessary to concentrate on the fundamental issues. Thus it might be justifiable to regard the veneration of saints as a fitting expression of Christianity, but one which belongs to the past and is no longer tenable today. The question is whether the somewhat sceptical Christians of today can so easily do away with the traditional veneration of saints. On the other hand, a deeper understanding of their faith might show that these traditions of the past also contain the seeds of the future.

Modern Christians who feel that praying to the saints has 'no meaning' for them must ask themselves whether they are not too conditioned by their own times or spiritually too narrow-minded and mean to describe themselves as true Christians. Christians of today should certainly not feel bound by a sense of traditionalism to include the veneration of saints as a matter of course in their religious practice. They should feel free to say that although they are prepared to acknowledge the historical significance, and to a certain extent also the example of the major Christian figures, both past and present, they nevertheless do not think that the individual feast days, pilgrimages, new canonizations, exhortations to pray to the saints (especially Mary), and so on, have any relevance for them.

People nowadays claim to be more self-critical and sceptical than in previous generations. We are more honest and questioning towards ourselves

and we are aware of the social, political and intellectual conditioning of man now and in the past.
Hence Christians should openly admit and even
seriously question their inability to venerate the
saints. They should not see this as inevitable or
self-justifying. Instead, they must ask themselves if
they can or should try to overcome it. Basically,
everyone must face this question as an individual;
nor may we simply come to the conclusion that
nothing can be done any more, or else the Church's
problems with regard to the veneration of saints
will not change within the foreseeable future.

Why shouldn't Christians be able to relate individually to the saints, even if the majority cannot or
do not wish to? At any rate it seems fitting today
that we should give some thought to the issue of
prayer to the saints. These reflections might throw
light on the reality and dimension of our faith, and
at the same time make us aware of its claims on us.
And one such demand is the veneration of the
saints, which is by no means as secondary as it
might at first seem.

2 · Why It Is Difficult Today to Pray to the Saints

Why is it that many or indeed the majority of practising Christians in the developed West who actively live their lives according to the intellectual and social ambiance of today cannot existentially cope with prayer to the saints (outside of the official liturgy of the Church)? The cause of this is probably extremely complex and difficult to grasp. We can perhaps single out two major reasons which in turn are intrinsically very complicated: one of a general human kind, and the other of a specifically religious or theological nature. I shall examine both of these reasons to see if they really justify the prevailing attitude of indifference, in both human and religious terms, to the dead.

37

Contemporary persons, those who are really part of today's world (and I mean this as a fact rather than a virtue), are strangely indifferent to the dead. People die, and are to the living, in the most literal sense, dead. The death announcements declare that the dead will not be forgotten, that they will continue to live in the memory of those who are left behind. This is probably as it should be in the intimate, personal sphere of family and friends. But it really has no bearing on the public, active aspects of life. There, the dead are dead and gone; they no longer have any significance in our lives. Even the pain of the bereaved which seems to bring back the dead is probably more likely to be the pain of loss affecting the ego. Some of the dead become objects of historical interest: for example, in editions of their literary bequests, in biographies and in history books. What concerns us in such cases is not the deceased themselves, but what happened in the past and how it affects us today. We are concerned with the details of their lives, recreating it in thought, but not with the deceased themselves. We place in cemeteries tombstones bearing the names of the dead, and it is astonishing how diligently graves are still cared for, how frequently people still visit the graves of their dead, especially on memorial and remembrance days.

This leads us to ask whether these manifestations are not a timid, embarrassed glimpse of our true feelings and fundamental humanity for which there is no scope or meaning in our everyday lives. If we are really honest with ourselves, these traces of a general cult of the dead are probably a remnant from the past which we continue to practise without knowing quite why, on the supposition that it will gradually die out because the real reasons for this kind of remembrance of the dead have long since vanished. For example, many people even today would be happy if they could bury their dead in a cemetery next to the church—as was always the case in rural communities in the past—in which they also celebrate the important ceremonies of their own lives. Then, on such occasions, they could visit the family grave and commemorate their dead. That is the truth: the dead are dead.

At this point I could of course go further and state that the reason why the dead no longer exist for us stems from the widespread belief (though one rarely admitted to individually) that there is no life after death. This may be the case. However, although this reason is the most important and complex of all, I cannot pursue it further here. For the purposes of this discussion I shall assume that Christians are convinced of the falseness and speciousness of this disbelief, or that they have the good will to dismiss the falseness and un-Christian nature of this disbelief and its irreconcilability with genuine Christian faith, professing instead a belief in eternal life which in the traditional sense of the Creed is a fundamental tenet of the Christian faith. But, even for Christians who do uphold this belief, indifference to the dead is still a very real problem.

Now, is this simply a 'fact' which we have to resign ourselves to, or even define and justify in terms of sceptical or materialist rationalism? If that is so, then it is not merely a 'fact', but a *question.* 'Facts' of an intellectual or political nature do of course carry weight, but they also raise questions which we have to judge and assess openly. They do not simply belong to the categorical law of our thoughts and actions; they can also be part of the dialectic of the historical process. Thus individuals are not empowered or obliged to attempt to overcome their own present. But there must be a general will to do so. For even if one fails one will have fulfilled the fundamental task of individual existence for which the basic responsibility must always be borne alone.

If I wished to scrutinize this 'fact' critically, I could of course conduct a general anthropological (metaphysical) and theological enquiry to question and dispute human certainty in general. In direct opposition to the mentality of today with its apparently unequivocal prejudices, I could consider one's real being as a person, as an absolutely free subject, as a being searching for the absolute mystery called God, and as the embodiment of absolute hope. And then I could pursue my investigation and see whether this total and true certainty, still part of our freedom as human beings, permits us this indifference towards the dead. However, this doubtless more reliable way of questioning the 'fact' is too long and too complex to undertake here. What I can do is to approach it from the opposite standpoint: in other words, to examine the inhumanity implied by our indifference towards the dead and how this seriously threatens our humanity which we feel to be such a central and crucial part of ourselves. This should give us a fuller, more truthful and fundamental understanding of ourselves as human beings.

Just what does this mean? Are we really being more pragmatic, more honest and more enlightened by not having a relationship to the dead? Just because we have lost something, does it necessarily mean that we can do without it forever? Surely life could have had customs and practices in the past which we have lost entirely or in part by seriously damaging our essential being? Shouldn't we at least assume that the past is superior to the present and that it contains, albeit in a new form, the true future? Perhaps this will help us in our search for a genuine relationship to the dead. At this point I can join forces with J. B. Metz (although this means extending the purely anthropological dimension to include theological considerations, since these will become relevant later on in our discussion):

'Seeing Jesus crucified and risen from the dead we hope that we, too, will be raised from the dead. The world we live in seems to be especially far removed from this secret hope of ours. We are presumably all too subject to the anonymous pressure of a social awareness that distances us more and more from belief in the raising of the dead, having already destroyed our feeling of contact and community with the dead. Of course we are still affected by pain and sorrow, melancholy and often unspeakable suffering at the inconsolable suffering of the dead. But our fear of death itself is stronger still, hence our insensitivity towards our dead relatives and friends. Too few of us empathize or identify with the dead. Thus we are not able to sense anything of their disappointment and silent protest at our indifference and over-hastiness to ignore them and concentrate only on the here and now.

'On the whole we are well able to protect ourselves against these and other similar problems. We either suppress them or denounce them as "unrealistic". But what do we mean here by "realism"? Is it simply the superficiality and shallowness of our unhappy consciousness and the banality of many of our cares? This "realism" clearly has its own taboos as a result of which sorrow is suppressed in our collective consciousness, melancholy is considered thoroughly suspect, and the problems of the dead are dismissed as futile and meaningless.

'But it is deeply inhuman to forget or suppress
the question of the needs of the dead. It implies
that we forget and suppress all past suffering and
that we submit without protest to the meaninglessness of all suffering. Finally, the happiness
of one generation can never make good the suffering of previous generations; thus no amount of
social progress can placate the injustice done to the
dead. If we go on too long submitting to the
meaninglessness of death and indifference to the
dead we shall end up having nothing but banal
hopes for the living as well. The growth of our
economic potential is, as we are constantly reminded, limited; it would seem that the potential
for meaning is also limited. It is as though the re-
serves are declining and that there is a danger that
the important concepts with which we describe our
own history—freedom, emancipation, justice,
happiness—will in the final analysis be reduced to
weak, insipid phrases' (German Synod text *Our
Hope*).

The magnificent combination of religious address
and theological reflection in this text speaks for itself and needs no further explanation or comment.
If we approach it with an open mind, we will acknowledge that in both human and Christian terms
our lives are inextricably bound to the dead, and
that this relationship would be meaningless if the
dead had simply disappeared into the void, if they
no longer existed. Just how this continuing solidarity with the dead can be realized will be considered

further on. At this point in our discussion it is only necessary to understand that the current indifference to the dead is anything but the glorious progress achieved by our times in defiance of the ancient, primitive traditions of the past; a progress which contemporary persons can only avoid by denying their being and their future existence.

To this I should like to add two small suggestions. Contemporary Catholic theology in Europe and North America shows little interest in the question of solidarity with the dead. We should not accept this as a matter of course. Hence, Helmut Peukert [1] adopts the methods of linguistic philosophy, epistemology, and other modern analytical procedures to examine the possible basis for a contemporary religious and theological language. Peukert's starting point and fundamental concept is the possibility of and need for an 'anamnetic, universal solidarity' which would include solidarity with the dead. Further discussion of this profoundly thoughtful book is beyond the scope of our present enquiry. But, clearly, when a book like this makes solidarity with the dead a fundamental theological issue, then conventional modern theologians must consider whether they are justified in largely overlooking it or at best

---

[1] *Wissenschaftstheorie—Handlungstheorie—Fundamentale Theologie. Analysen zu Ansatz und Status theologischer Theoriebildung* (Dusseldorf 1976).

tolerating it as an insignificant side-issue, or whether their lack of attention is not simply a tribute to the superficial mentality of today which Christian theology is fundamentally bound to come to terms with critically, especially at a time when this theology is trying to show that it is politically and socially critical and responsible.

Another comment: it is perhaps conceivable that Christian theology in Africa, if it wishes to become truly African, will introduce a new, independent form of ancestor worship, and that from there it might be imported into Christian theology in the rest of the world. It would be extremely regrettable and ominous for the future of Christian theology as a whole if this African contribution were to meet with nothing but indifference from the rest of the Christian world.

This brings me to the second reason for our indifference towards the dead, one which implies a religious and theological problem over and above the decline in human involvement with the dead. This is the question of praying to the saints; one, therefore, of a specifically religious and Christian relationship to the dead, of whether we may invoke them and trust in their intercession (whatever these terms mean to us precisely). This question certainly presents us today with difficulties and inhibitions which we cannot overcome even by establishing, or desiring to establish, a close feeling of solidarity with the dead. What precisely are these religious and theological difficulties connected with prayer to the saints?

Nowadays our relationship to God is marked by a feature which has not always been so apparent in the past, even leaving aside the threat posed to this relationship today by atheism and the way this affects the atmosphere of Christian life. We experience God as an ineffable, unfathomable mystery to whom we are nevertheless bound by all the special characteristics of human existence (intellect, freedom, hope, love, the loneliness of individual responsibility, the consequence and incomprehensibility of our humanity, and death). Yet in the end we encounter God speechless, in a state of submission which we are unable to control or comprehend (though also filled with a final hoping trust). For this reason, we get the impression that *the* genuine religious feeling, which cannot be demythologized or psychologically and socio-critically destroyed, can only be realized in this act of final, hoping surrender, submitting ourselves to this silent mystery which shelters, forgives, saves and fulfils us only if it is embraced unconditionally.

Today we feel that everything still connected with traditional religious practice and Christianity is too far removed from the bottomless profundity of our own religious experience. Therefore we are very critical towards those aspects of traditional religiosity which approach these depths in any way. We are tempted to analyze them psychologically, sociologically, aesthetically and historically and to dismiss them as temporary, finite, changeable and conditional. By these means we are able to see them merely as concrete manifestations of our own finite existence which we silently abandon to the unfathomable mystery in which we have unconditionally placed all our hopes. Finally, we see the modern destruction of all concrete forms of religion as part of the same universal 'sacrifice' in which we yield to nameless mystery. (No wonder we feel secretly drawn to the figures of Eastern religion with their expressions of smiling submission to the ineffable mystery.)

Where do the dead fit in? Can we really call out to them once they have crossed the one true threshold which we prepare ourselves to cross when they have left us; where day and night, yes and no are one and the same thing; where we no longer dare to differentiate since it would bring us back to where we are? Even if our hope for the dead and thus for ourselves signifies that they are saved for all eternity, this does not mean that they have withdrawn from us into a dimension in which we can no longer identify them. They have not been 'decomposed' by the earth, but by God himself. Finite beings, in spite of the positive quality we so desperately ascribe to their finiteness, cease to be substantial once they no longer exist at a distance from God, who seems to be their salvation, once they become immersed in God's infinity. How can we still invoke individual names when addressing a world in which individuality no longer exists, but only the silence of God?

3 · Praying to the Saints as Intercessors with God

The difficulties of invoking the help of the saints in prayer can perhaps be illustrated by referring to traditional concepts and axioms. In Christian theology a truly religious, salvific act is necessarily one which, with God's merciful intercession, is directed towards and accepts God in his utmost reality. The inner principle and the ultimate aim of every genuinely religious act is God in all his reality. This means that, at least in a certain sense, it would not be possible for any human being to intercede with God in the religious act. For God is not reached from a distance *through* a created reality as if through a reprimand communicated by God but not intrinsically part of him; instead, God is experienced directly. But of course we can speak of human intercession in the religious act for the simple reason that the subject of such an act, the finite human being, cannot be excluded from it. He or she is also endowed with certain qualifications essential to an act of direct communion with God.

There must be certain kinds of human intercession with God, both of an inward nature (grace acquired) and an outward nature (the human language of revelation, the sacraments, and so on). But these elements do not come *between* God and the subject on whom grace is bestowed; rather, they are the prerequisites for (and eventually the consequences of) one's direct relationship with God. I cannot expand further here on human immediacy to God, which is stated in the Catholic doctrine of forgiveness, and is crucial for an understanding of the religious act as an instrument of salvation. This makes it all the more urgent to ask how a saint, who is a finite being, can be part of a religious act; how we can pray to a saint, not simply as a prerequisite or secondary factor of the religious act, but as the aim or object of our prayer.

If prayer is to be a religious act in the strict sense of the word, everything finite must vanish, in spite of the finite nature of the individual performing the act, so that we can accept directly and devoutly our only salvation: God in all his reality. If communication is established directly with God in prayer, how do the saints fit in? Does a saint have any 'influence' on our prayers? Can we invoke his or her intercession when we have already entered into the most holy of infinities? Surely the Catholic doctrine of forgiveness, in its very essence, implies the abolition of the concept of the heavenly hierarchy of angels and saints in which the lower orders can only aspire to rise in the hierarchy by means of the intercession of those higher up. The problem is to find an appropriate way of answering these questions.

4 · Love of God and Love of Our Neighbour Closely Linked

In the hope of making further headway with this question, let us start with a doctrine of the Christian faith that may at first sight seem to have little bearing on it. This is the unity of love of God and love of our neighbour. However, I shall not simply repeat the usual comments made on this subject. There is real unity in the mutual causal relationship between these two concepts. To love our neighbour is not merely a moral stipulation deriving from the love of God, with the injunction that we cannot really love God unless we also fulfil his commandment to love our neighbour. The unity between love of God and love of neighbour is much more fundamental, as I shall attempt to show.

Despite the nearness to God which is brought about through loving him, there is a kind of love of God which automatically includes the love of our neighbour. The reasons for this I can only summarize here, though I can indicate further material for consideration. To start with, we should not naively assume that the most basic and essential religious acts are always of an explicitly religious nature. In a genuine and lasting sense, all religious acts are imparted in a secular form (the characteristics of which will shortly be discussed) and do not necessarily have to be religious in theme in order to present God himself in explicit, concrete form. To put it simply, when a person loves someone absolutely, unconditionally and freely, trusting completely in the unknowable risk of loving unconditionally as being the final hope of saving himself or herself, God is at least implicitly affirmed as the source of such love. And, through God's constant mercy which is conveyed by such love, God becomes part of the loving person, justifying the act and bringing him or her salvation. Given that we can only realize our potential as human beings by freely participating in the world around us, such acts of loving clearly have an existential priority over specifically religious acts; in fact, such loving can even be seen as a religious act of a general nature. (This statement is really just an existential definition of the traditional precept that we encounter God through the world, and that this is a necessary prerequisite for faith.)

Clearly, therefore, we must distinguish between explicit religious acts and those which are fundamentally human in character. In no circumstances should the human and religious significance of this distinction be underestimated or disregarded. But at the same time we must acknowledge that the act of loving God is closely related to the act of loving our neighbour, that these acts are mutually coexistent. We should always bear in mind that the God in all his reality to whom we reach out through our freely given acts of love is a God of love, of supremely free love. Hence we cannot accept and affirm him simply by loving him; we must also freely love and accept all other spiritual beings to whom he lovingly reveals himself.

These reflections should help us to understand how human beings (and hence love for them) can lead us to God and his love, without however coming between God and us. In other words, the persons we love form a direct line of communication to God. The world is always the starting point for our relationship to God because we can only build up this relationship freely and consciously out of our own finite existence. The aim of the religious act is not that we be consumed or subsumed, but that we should attain to the highest level of reality and independence. But to achieve this we need a mediator who in the most literal sense 'intercedes' without disturbing the immediacy of our relationship to God. If we take 'human being' instead of 'world' as our starting point, bearing in mind that one can only realize one's true being, freely responsible to God, with the help of one's fellow men, we can say that the person who is the object of our love is the real mediator in our relationship to God, that through him or her we achieve direct contact with God. This intercession is not to be thought of as hierarchical or graduated; rather, it is based on the insight that one is only freely in possession of one's own being, which in turn is to be entrusted to God, when and if one surrenders oneself to love for another being. Just how explicitly this love of our fellow human beings is related to the sense of immediacy to God in the religious act is a totally different matter. However, regardless of individual differences in religious practice, the basic correlation between love of God and love of our neighbour remains.

Given the different spiritual needs of persons it is inevitable, and indeed legitimate, that they should have different ways of expressing the various elements which constitute a religious act. Thus it is possible that persons who love their fellow human beings unconditionally are in fact loving

God directly, even though they may be unaware of the theological implications of this. On the other hand, it is also possible that those who with God's grace succeed in transcending themselves and approaching God directly in a more or less unstructured act are nevertheless people who love their fellow human beings; and it is as such that they approach the abyss of the unfathomable mystery to which they submit in love and hope. These possible variations in approach and intention do not affect the fundamental unity of love of God and love of our fellow humans. Each one of us must find the approach best suited to our personality and destiny with the help of God's will and our own freedom of choice. But it would be unnatural for any of us to exclude our fellow human beings categorically from the immediacy of our relationship with God, or for that matter to exclude God from our relationship with others by focussing our entire existence on this world.

Having said all this, it is still not clear why and how a prayer of intercession by someone else and a plea for such intercession do not interfere with the immediacy of the religious act. One thing should be clear by now: namely, that only persons who love others and include them lovingly in their lives can truly achieve this immediacy to God. But I shall return to a more detailed discussion of this point later on. At this stage in my reflections, I can say that when and if other people seem to be 'forgotten' in the inherent intensity of the religious act it is really the self that is forgotten. In what is above all a mystical phenomenon individuals completely forget and subsume themselves in order to realize their true being. To think it would be easier to forget the other person than to forget oneself in the genuine religious act is an easily understandable delusion caused by the primitive nature of one's objectifying consciousness. But if we think that we can only forget ourselves through loving others, that we can only reach God by breaking through our egoism and loving others, then we must reverse the statement. In a certain sense it is easier to forget ourselves in a truly religious act than it is to forget other people.

5 · Venerating the Saints by Loving Our Neighbour in and with Christ

I could of course consider quite different aspects of the Christian faith in order to come to a closer understanding of this direct intercession with God. I could mention the incarnate structure of the Christian world-view, culminating in the doctrine of the hypostatic union between the Logos and Christ's human reality. Christ's human reality, with the word, the sacraments and the Church leading from it, is the true mediator in our relationship to God. But it does not really intervene *between* us and God as a connecting link, any more than we could imagine something 'between' the Word and Christ's human reality. Similarly, the divine testimony of the Word by definition excludes any thought of it as a human mediator between God and Christ. Hence Christ's human reality is the prerequisite making it possible for us to have a direct relationship to God. Through him and his immediacy to God we are granted an eternal validity that is finally confirmed by his death and resurrection.

Therefore it is clear that the ability to mediate or intercede must be seen as a factor in the constitution of human beings. They must be intrinsically able to communicate directly with God, though this is not something automatically granted to every person in every instance. They must be able to transcend themselves, and to approach God as free spirits. Thus the question of direct intercession with God depends on the qualities which persons must freely possess if they are to be able to receive God's direct self-revelation. According to Christian doctrine, one of these qualities is human solidarity with Jesus and Jesus' solidarity with all of humanity. God gives himself directly to humanity (in the form of the offer of freedom and of God's offer of victory) because he wills it, and because this will to reveal himself has become irreversibly and also historically tangible through Christ's death and resurrection. From this we can go on to say that God wants individuals to receive his direct revelation, in so far as they belong to that humanity in which

God's revelation manifested itself triumphantly through Jesus Christ.

In other words, individuals are suitable subjects to receive God's direct revelation provided they are firmly united to their fellow humans who triumphantly acknowledge God's revelation through Christ. Human beings are only able to communicate directly with God in 'the communion of saints' (in and with Jesus Christ). This communion of saints is a necessary form of intercession between humanity and God. It does not actually come between humanity and God, but is an indispensable part of the human subject who is able to receive this direct revelation. That being so, we can say that the veneration of saints is nothing other than the outward expression of this communion of saints through whom we all have direct access to God. Hence praying to the saints is not an additional task for Christians over and above their relationship to God. Whether the saints should be venerated in an official, ritualistic way remains to be seen.

To sum up the discussion so far: All Christians venerate the saints (as regards the fundamental theological structure of this veneration), at least to the extent that they love their fellow humans (whom they encounter concretely) with love which acts as a necessary form of mediation for their relationship to God. When we speak of venerating the saints, we simply mean that love of our fellow humans is extended to include all, not only those people we actually meet in our everyday lives. Truly Christian love of our fellow human beings must embrace *all,* including the dead. Only when the person loved has finally overcome the ambivalence of his or her existence and is safely held for eternity in God's love can our love for him or her be freed of its inevitable limitations. The Christian mystery of being directly in the presence of God is certainly not a religious solipsism. It does not allow us to lose ourselves in God's incomprehensible ineffability and inestimability. On the contrary, it saves us, because the God in whom this mystery is lovingly subsumed is the God who also wanted us to lose ourselves freely in our love for our fellow human beings. People who find themselves by losing themselves in God, in whom God becomes everything, are not isolated selves; rather, it is precisely through loving their neighbour that they establish the truth of their individual selves. The communion of saints, and consequently the veneration of the saints, is a central factor in our direct relationship to God: a way of bringing us directly into God's presence.

6 · Venerating the Saints Is Synonymous with the Adoration of God

But does this really solve our problem? It would not seem to be the case. For even if we say that when we pray directly to God our fellow human beings are indissolubly united to us in love, and that this solidarity is the prerequisite for every truly religious act, this still does not make it sufficiently clear that we can call on the saints and ask for their intercession. It seems that when we do this we are once again inserting a mediating factor between us and God, which we had previously tried to avoid, and this seems to remove the reality of the religious act.

How should we approach this? Perhaps we

should simply say that praying to the saints is a secondary, derivative analogy to a religious act which has nothing to do with the essential nature of the religious act. Perhaps we should point out that there are many legitimate human acts which lack the fundamental quality of the truly religious act, yet are justified by their essential humanity. For example, love of our fellow human beings, human intercommunication and solidarity, and so on. Perhaps we could extend the concept of communication between people to include the dead, and thus find a solution to our problem? Perhaps we should appeal to traditional theology to acknowledge and emphasize the difference between the adoration of God (*latreia*) and the veneration of the saints (*doulia*), which is not a form of adoration, but is nevertheless legitimate and meaningful? But even these suggestions and distinctions would not solve our difficulties. If we, rightly, include the dead in the concept of legitimate human and universal communication, we have by definition made a basic human ontological assumption about the veneration of the saints which must now be acknowledged and taken into account. But this appeal for what might be called 'ancestor worship' does not explain how invoking the dead could possibly be a genuine religious act. This raises the perpetual question of whether we may distinguish between adoration and veneration in such a way that this invocation can in fact constitute a religious act in the full sense of the word.

The question is therefore as follows: Can there be religious acts aimed directly at God, though not so explicitly or thematically as in the perfect and fundamental religious act? If so, they should be seen not just as the rudiments of the basic religious act, or as forms of lament; rather, their lasting significance should be sought in the innumerable different ways human beings have of fulfilling themselves. I must now try to elucidate this statement more fully, even if it means repeating certain points already covered.

As previously noted in our discussion about the unity of our love for God and for our fellow human beings, God can only be loved through our love for our neighbour. Furthermore, if we love our neighbour unconditionally, we are necessarily affirming God as the cause of this love, since it emanates from God's revelation of himself to us. In either case this love can be given formal expression, though this need not happen. Thus some religious acts which relate directly to God do not in fact express this openly and clearly. This of course in no way invalidates those explicitly religious acts in which the fundamental character of the act is developed to the full. On the other hand, this does not mean that human beings, given the plurality of their nature, could or should dismiss these informally conceived yet nevertheless genuine religious acts in order to concentrate on the intense reality of the most explicit religious acts. For example, we cannot say that we love God only within the concentrated experience of the religious act, and that this contains in a superior way what people in the distraction of their everyday lives describe as love for their fellow humans. Since humans are finite, pluralistic beings they must continually develop the various dimensions of their existence, confident that in this way they will find the true God; the God, that is, who wills and loves this plurality, and only gives himself entirely to those who have accepted this innate diversity and thus affirm the multiplicity of religious acts which only God can unite through absolute human love for him. This is why Christian doctrine has always humbly maintained a legitimate variety of religious acts (love of God and fear of God, joy and sorrow, mourning and jubilation, and so on) and has refused to combine this plurality of human existence and all its corresponding religious acts in one single total act. That is the ideal proclaimed by quietism and other radical spiritual movements, thus unintentionally giving the final honour to humanity rather than to God.

Humans must accept the plurality of their being confidently, and without fearing that because of it they will lose God in all his uniqueness and immeasurability.

Humans are historical beings. For this reason we do not possess the fulness of our reality at any one time; we do not have the power to overcome our historically diffused plurality of being. We hope with justification that at death our total historical reality will be gathered together in one act, similar to the way in which God possesses the total fulness of his reality simultaneously (even though the medieval theologians also discreetly reflected on the possible diversity of the saints' acts in eternity).

Even when we act of our own free will, our actions are implicitly related to God himself, regardless of whether they are in fact directed towards another 'object'. This is because our specific acts are always fused with our plurality by the fundamental unity of our existence as sanctified spirits. Hence, although the traditional teaching of the Church rightly distinguishes between worshiping God and venerating the saints, this does not mean that these two acts are merely superficially complementary to one another. The act of venerating the saints (that is, our freely realized communion with them) is also by implication an act of worship to God, and therefore constitutes a genuine religious act without in any way disturbing the immediacy of our relationship to God.

7 · How Do We Petition the Saints for Intercession?

As I have shown, nothing can come 'between' God and us. On the other hand, one of the conditions for this closeness to God is that we should belong to the communion of the saints. But perhaps this still does not make it quite clear how the communion of the saints, which can certainly be effected by means of a specific, explicit act, can take the concrete form of appealing to the saints to ask for their intercession. Although this communion with the saints is included in the official liturgy of the Church, the saints themselves are not addressed directly. Why? How can this still be possible? No clear-cut answer has so far been found to this question, chiefly because we cannot take it for granted that we can address the saints directly simply because they exist, as is attempted in spiritualist gatherings.

The following short anecdote might help us to proceed in our investigations. When I was in Rome during the Council I had the opportunity, together with a group of others, to meet the great Protestant theologian Karl Barth. Our discussion turned to the veneration of the Virgin. I asked Karl Barth whether an individual may ask another Christian to pray for him. After a short hesitation, he replied that the individual should ask his fellow Christian to pray *with* him. The conversation then moved on to other topics. I admit that for many years I thought Barth's answer was intentionally evasive, that he wished to avoid the issue of veneration of the Virgin. Now I wonder if we should not pursue his point.

To start with, there is nothing new about the saints' intercession on our behalf with God. On the contrary it is central to their entire history and to eternal salvation; they rest in God's presence yet are also joined in perpetual communion with us. Their intercession for us depends of course on the degree of intensity, explicit or otherwise, with which we participate in this act of communion, which in turn reflects on our relationship to God. The saints pray 'with us' and thus 'for us'. Our plea for their intercession is not therefore an attempt to create some new, individualistic kind of spiritualistic communication. The concrete reality of the communion of saints exists already, and through it we worship God. It is the practical realization of this communion which freely embraces a wide variety of religious acts. Hence it can include a petition for intercession, while still remaining essentially the faithful realization of the communion of saints in which we stand before God, and in which we may expect his mercy and help. Seen in these terms, calling on the saints for their intercession in no way interposes 'between' us and God. On the contrary it provides concrete evidence of the fact that God loves each one of us as a unique being. He loves every single being he has created, and forms us into a community in which we can all love one another. We do not invoke the help of the saints because otherwise they would not intercede on our behalf; rather, in their eternal salvation they do nothing but intercede for us. In praying to the saints we show that we believe in this perpetual intercession because it enables us to accept and make use of its beneficial effects.

8 · The Salvific Role of the Saints

Having grasped these factors concerned with invoking the intercession of the saints, it is however possible for the persons concerned to be aware that the particular saint (for instance, the Virgin Mary) whom they are calling on had (and has) a more important function in the history of salvation, and thus in eternity, than is appropriate to their request. The teaching of the Catholic Church openly acknowledges such discrepancies. Heaven, despite universal perfection, is not envisaged by the Church as a uniform mass of identical souls; hence there is no fear of 'envy' on the part of those who fell short and who might be expected to envy those who finally reached a 'higher' degree of holiness and thus a greater happiness and proximity to God. Inadequate though such quantitative concepts may be, the traditional doctrine of the Church remains impartial towards the varying degrees of blessedness achieved by those who have been saved. This differentiation is due first and foremost to the qualitative incomparability of their lives as a whole, which by extension implies that there should be differences in importance within the communion of saints. But these are not seen as unfairly favouring one over the other, because each is filled with the most selfless love towards all the others, and this causes him to experience the possibly greater significance of his neighbour as his own happiness.

Hence it is quite possible and legitimate for the persons who invoke the intercession of a specific saint to do so with the conviction that their plea will be listened to according to the unique significance and role of the relevant saint in the history of salvation. This conviction acknowledges openly that the communion of saints to whom such a plea is directed is not a faceless mass of 'equals' but the communion of those who have been saved for eternity, each one of whom has a different and unique significance for us all. This enables us to understand how certain saints are regarded as 'patrons' (the founders of religious orders, donators of local churches, and so on), if this patronage can be seen as a specific function attributed to the saint in

church history. By extension, it would be absolutely reasonable for individual Christians to revere
privately, as 'patrons' of their religious experiences,
certain people who have played important roles in
their religious lives.

9 · Commemorating a Saint as a Patron

In Catholic piety there are special patron saints for churches, for individual groups or countries, for religious communities, for certain professions, and so on. The Pope also officially designates certain saints as protective patrons. But this in no way means that the Pope exercises any kind of jurisdiction over the dead. (In fact it is a basic theological precept that granting dispensations for the dead does not constitute a lawful act in the same way as it does where the living are concerned.)

The nomination of a saint as a protective patron simply means that the head of the Church permits and recommends certain groups in the official body of the faithful to offer a specific saint their explicit veneration. But, in any case, these patrons can be seen as concrete symbols of our solidarity with the dead in heaven, united before God. It is our duty to love those who are far away from us, but that love becomes real and concrete through our love for those around us. Hence the communion of the saints, who make it possible for us to communicate directly with God, is in no sense an abstract or theoretical phenomenon. Quite the reverse: It becomes a concrete reality uniting us with everyone connected with our lives, closely or otherwise, who has gone before us and now rests in the peace of God.

Hence it is up to each one of us to choose our own particular patrons, who may of course be those officially nominated by the Church. If someone feels, on the basis of personal experience, that St. Anthony of Padua gives him or her particular confidence in God's providence, especially when he or she has lost something, we should not immediately object to this as superstition. This kind of subjective link between the recollection of a saint and trust in God's providence can be applied equally to the insignificant events of daily life. However, if this is taken to an extreme, then the relevant saints are being considered in terms of a very limited sphere of competence which the petitioner must know about and apply to a specific aim in order to achieve the desired result. This amounts to superstition, and must be avoided by Christians at all costs.

After this doubtless somewhat lengthy reflection on the theological basis for venerating and praying to the saints, I must now show how these theoretical considerations actually apply to the Christian life, though, of course, these theories cannot replace the actual experience of praying to the saints which each believer must achieve on his or her own.

10 · Cultivating Our Solidarity with the Dead

To begin with, it has to be admitted that the difficulties, both human and religious, which I outlined earlier cannot ever be completely solved by theoretical means. The feeling that the dead are so terribly remote from us and that we and all of our contemporaries will be overwhelmed if we dare to broach this disturbing mystery in the religious act makes it almost impossible, or at any rate too troublesome, for us to pray to the saints. These feelings do not vanish just because I have attempted to establish a theological basis for prayer to the saints. Indeed, such feelings should not simply vanish, because they are an essential, authentic part of our relationship to God. Thus, we can say definitively that we should not pray to the saints in order to find a compromise solution to the problem of our relationship to the dead; rather, our desire to pray to the saints should emerge *from* these feelings.

When at the moment of death people submit unconditionally to the incomprehensible, unfathomable mystery of God, they must be aware of what they are giving up to the eternal mystery, they must see themselves as the ones who are vanishing. Thus, in the final religious act, individuals must be conscious of themselves in an extraordinary way. Then they do not experience this last act as lonely, isolated subjects, but as persons communicating with all other human beings through selfless love, yielding up their humanity to the eternal God. In this way they participate in Christ's last act in which he too submitted to the Father, thereby achieving his final, perfect union with God. In this last religious act individuals are not subsumed in God as isolated beings, but as representatives of the whole of humanity, of all of the living. Therefore, individuals and mankind as a whole are extinguished simultaneously. And this is precisely the starting point for the final salvation of each individual in unison with all of mankind, following the example of Christ's death and resurrection.

As already stated, this does not necessarily mean that the element of union of the self with humanity has to be explicitly embodied in every basic religious act, or that it can always be present in finite, historically rooted human consciousness. But the 'veneration of the saints' as defined above is a vital element in the religious act because solidarity with the 'saints' (and hence their loving veneration) is essential if humanity is to be able to give itself up to God. Only those who can love always and everywhere can achieve this final submission. It therefore seems obvious, and meaningful, that we should gain a clearer understanding of this essential feature of the religious act, namely the veneration of the saints.

Our main problem with regard to the practice of praying to the saints is not so much, or at any rate not exclusively, of a theological nature. This aspect I have discussed in considerable detail above. Our real difficulty lies in our general lack of human solidarity with the dead. For this solidarity is a necessary prerequisite if we are to venerate the saints honestly and genuinely, not merely according to some official cult established by the Church. Our relationship to the dead should not be misinterpreted in parapsychological or spiritualistic terms, as outlined in the foregoing discussion. Nor should it be seen as a phenomenon about which we register nothing but its presence or absence. Our religious duty demands that we do not simply hide behind a supposed failure in our relationship to the dead. It is a duty we can cultivate if we choose, for we have been granted the freedom to discover our reality or to fail to do so, and the same applies to our relationship to the dead. In this context we might well refer back to Johann Metz's remarks in Part I of this book.

We cannot freely commemorate the dead if we are merely holding on to the past with combined compulsion and curiosity. True remembrance of the dead enables us to protect the deepest reality of our existence (which cannot be thought of in individualistic terms), and to carry it into the future as our legacy and duty. Although we should remember all of the dead, we should nevertheless concentrate primarily on two groups of people. First, we should remember those who have been close to us, who have loved us, whom we loved ourselves, and towards whom we perhaps still feel terribly guilty (despite the fact that the dead can no longer enforce this guilt), so that we have to live with their silent, constantly reiterated forgiveness.

We are bound to our deceased relations by many valid ties which could and should develop into a continually growing sense of solidarity. We should not see them as dead, but as living beings who have taken their relationship to us with them into eternity. G. C. Lichtenberg, although a 'freethinker' and rationalist, continued into old age to commemorate quietly the anniversary of his beloved mother's death. It was not just a vestige of archaicism or folklore still present in this sceptical rationalist. Rather, it was the concrete realization of a truth which we too must continually regain for ourselves, regardless of what the supposedly educated people of today may think. Though of course they do still—contrary to their enlightened superficiality—erect tombstones on their relations' graves, which ultimately, given their attitude, is meaningless. Perhaps the easiest way of remembering the dead who have been close to us is to remind ourselves what we owe them, how we are indebted to them in a debt of love which can only be settled by that never-ending, forgiving love we call God.

Second, we should remember all those who have faded into the oblivion of history. They too (not just the great figures of world history) should be given a special place in our commemoration of the dead. But then, even with the great, we do not know for certain if the eternal yield of their lives is particularly large, or whether in this respect they in fact belong to the vast army of insignificant, apparently unimportant souls. We must remember the humble and the despised, those who were of no apparent significance, those who died young, and those who have vanished anonymously in the blind cruelty of history. We should not remember only the pharaohs who built the pyramids, but also those who with great pain and distress heaved the stones until they died ignominiously. We should not commemorate only those whom history calls the victors, but also the losers who, true to their duty and their conscience, died ingloriously, as well as those who met their end in the hell of the concentration camps, children tortured to death, and so on.

It would be both sceptical and egotistical to question the purpose of commemorating the unknown. Must it serve a purpose in order to be meaningful and necessary? This surely is what humanity should be about. Surely it helps us to face God and eternity if we remind outselves continually of the dead, affirming their reality in faith, hope and love. This also gives a deeper meaning to the apparently bizarre habit that many pious Christians have of praying for and to the forgotten 'poor souls'.

Remembering the dead in this way automatically becomes a prayer even if it does not contain a specific petition to the 'saints', a plea for their intercession. When we recall the dead they take us to a certain extent into their sphere, drawing us into their silence; they dispel the noisy bustle of the world and enable us to face the events of our lives with a calmness which makes it possible for us to pray. Prayer certainly requires the silence of solitude, and this is intensified rather than diminished when we withdraw slightly from the everyday world to think of the dead, anticipating our own death, as far as possible, as the release through which God is finally revealed to us.

In fact, praying to individual saints is secondary to this general remembrance of the dead, which, as a result of our hope for universal salvation, is simultaneously a commemoration of the (largely anonymous) body of all the saints. In comparison, the remembrance of a specific saint is like a request for some practical necessity (our daily bread), which is an aspect of our prayer for salvation, which is God himself. In both cases the actual petition is a legitimate expression of our calm, obedient acceptance of the irreconcilable diversity of our existence, as finite beings, without wanting to press the 'whole' of our religious existence into a single moment. But if such acts are to be truly religious we must perform them in a state of grace in which we come to face God in unity with all the dead (including those to come), trusting unconditionally (in this communion of the saints) that God will reveal himself to us in all his glory.